C-1

THE SLIPPERS' KEEPER

IAN WALLACE

GROUNDWOOD BOOKS   HOUSE OF ANANSI PRESS   TORONTO   BERKELEY

Special thanks to Leisa Purdon, Joe's granddaughter,
for her dogged research on my behalf.
Big hugs to Madeleine and Margot Blake-McLaughlin
for their winning smiles.

Groundwood Books / House of Anansi Press
110 Spadina Avenue, Suite 801, Toronto, Ontario M5V 2K4
or c/o Publishers Group West
1700 Fourth Street, Berkeley, CA 94710

We acknowledge for their financial support of our publishing program the
Canada Council for the Arts, the Government of Canada through the Canada
Book Fund (CBF) and the Ontario Arts Council.

Canada Council   Conseil des Arts
for the Arts   du Canada

ONTARIO ARTS COUNCIL
CONSEIL DES ARTS DE L'ONTARIO
an Ontario government agency
un organisme du gouvernement de l'Ontario

Library and Archives Canada Cataloguing in Publication
Wallace, Ian, author, illustrator
The slippers' keeper / written and illustrated by Ian Wallace.
Issued in print and electronic formats.
ISBN 978-1-55498-414-5 (bound).—ISBN 978-1-55498-415-2 (pdf)
1. Purdon, Joe, 1914-1982—Juvenile literature. 2. Slipper
orchids—Protection—Ontario—Juvenile literature.
3. Conservationists—Canada—Biography—Juvenile literature.
I. Title.
QH31.P87W34 2015   j333.72092   C2014-905798-9
C2014-905799-7

The illustrations were done in watercolor
and pencil on Arches watercolor paper.
Design by Michael Solomon
Printed and bound in Malaysia

MIX
Paper from
responsible sources
FSC® C012700

In memory of Joe
and to Rhodena,
who opened the door to me
so graciously,
with gratitude

THE SLIPPERS' KEEPER

JOE PURDON didn't enjoy working the family farm. As quick as his chores were done, he would strike out with his dog, Laddie, and together they would trek the three hundred acres of bush and fen nestled deep in the hardscrabble highlands of Eastern Ontario. Over time, he came to know every hill and glen, every genus of tree and plant, every beaver dam and osprey nest, wolf and black bear den, where the deer slept and the moose and coyotes ventured, where the carp and bass spawned and the turtles, frogs and toads laid their eggs, the arc of the sun and the phases of the moon.

One June day, when he was thirteen years old, Joe came upon a cluster of eight rare wild orchids standing tall in the fen's peaty earth. He had noticed the plants on previous treks, but he had never seen any in bloom. Crouching low, he cupped a flower in the palm of his hand. It was as soft and delicate as the inside of Laddie's ears.

"Aren't you the prettiest thing this side of sunset?" he said.

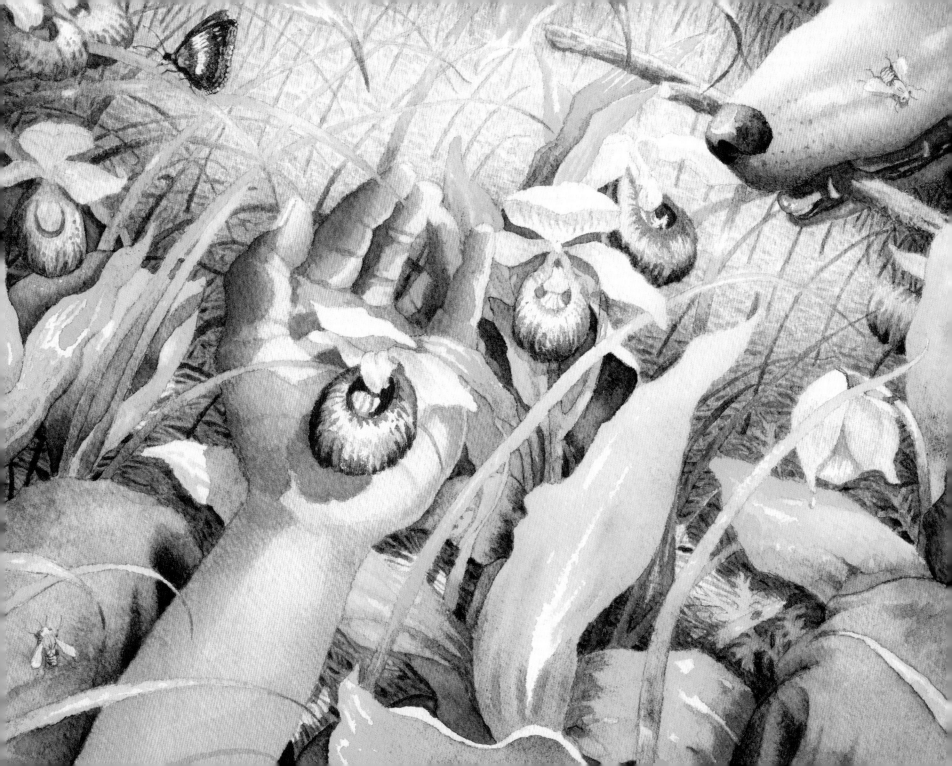

Only four days before, his teacher, Miss McIntyre, had discovered two plants blooming at the edge of the schoolyard, and she had taken her students to see them.

"What you are looking at is a wonder," she said. "The Showy Lady's Slipper doesn't have a nectar and can't pollinate itself, so it depends on an inquisitive bee or insect stumbling into its pouch."

Joe swatted away a deer fly for the umpteenth time that afternoon.

"As remarkable, it takes seven to fifteen years for a plant to bloom even though it produces fifteen to thirty-five thousand seeds in a single pod every year. Can you imagine that?"

Several of her students shook their heads, several sighed and someone quipped, "That's a mother lode of seeds, miss!"

The deer fly came back with dogged persistence. Joe smacked it dead against his neck.

"…and if that wasn't difficulty enough," he recalled Miss McIntyre saying, "they need just the right balance of water and sunlight. Too much water and they drown. Too little and they die."

"They sure are pernickety," one of his classmates said.

"And they sure could use some help," said his best friend, Scott.

"They could indeed," said Miss McIntyre.

Joe looked about the fen. "Are there more of you? Or are you the only ones?" He turned to Laddie. "I guess we'll have to find out, won't we, boy?"

Throughout the afternoon, they searched for other plants in bloom. To Joe's surprise they discovered sixteen more.

"Wonders are sprouting everywhere, Laddie!"

Dinnertime would be upon them soon so they headed for home, but the orchids stuck like nettles in Joe's mind. He promised himself that he would return and continue the search.

In the summer days that followed, Joe and Laddie trekked the fen in every spare moment.

"And thirty-two makes fifty-six," he said two weeks later.

He stroked Laddie's head, remembering Miss McIntyre's words. And then he asked himself, What if…? By the time he reached the barn, a daring idea had taken hold of his imagination.

Excitedly, Joe told his family of his discovery and what he wanted to do.

"You want to help wild orchids grow in the fen!" his father exclaimed. "If it's work you're after there's plenty just beyond the kitchen door!"

His sister, Mary, snickered.

"Hush now," chided their mother.

"But the orchids are part of our farm, too, Dad. They just happen to be in the fen. And they need more help than potatoes."

"And that swamp hasn't nourished even one potato that anyone could eat or sell since a glacier covered this land."

"Now, Rufus," interrupted his mother. "The boy needs to pursue his own interests beyond farm work. Something that will bring him pleasure."

"Pleasure!" his father harrumphed. "We'd all enjoy some pleasure! But pleasure won't put food on the table or keep the roof over our heads, if *the boy* hasn't noticed."

A frosty chill fell over the dinner table.

"Can I do it when my chores and schoolwork are done?" Joe asked.

His father chewed on a boiled potato. "But only then."

After the dishes had been washed and the cows had been milked, Joe took his mother and sister to see the rare wild orchids. Laddie came, too. They strode quickly. Night was settling comfortably into the sun-drenched hills.

"They look prehistoric," said Mary. "Like Ma's slippers. Only tinier and with wings."

Their mother chortled. "And each one would fit just one of my fat, stubby toes!"

The next morning, Joe began to read everything he could about the Showy Lady's Slipper. Miss McIntyre helped him in his search, and with her guidance they developed a plan.

Every other day, Joe returned to the fen where he monitored the water levels.

He removed branches and trees from the beaver dam, releasing just the right amount of water into the pond along the fen's western edge.

With a twig in hand, he pollinated plants and nudged seeds from their pods, nesting them in the peaty earth.

He cut away scrub brush and transplanted the orchids, moving them from heavy shade into sunnier spots.

Often, when he returned, the beavers had filled in the new gaps in the dam. But Joe didn't mind. He understood that they were protecting their home.

All the while, he chased away deer that came to feast on the orchids and battled swarms of deer flies and mosquitoes that came to feast on him.

"Someday," he said, "there'll be more slippers in the fen than there are bugs in the bush." And he whistled through his teeth.

When winter dawned, he thinned the birch and ash trees, the cedars and tamaracks, letting warm sunlight shine on the snow-covered ground. The felled trees he hauled home behind Major, his horse.

Later, the trees were sawed into boards at the mill down the road. With his father's help, Joe crafted the boards into rowboats, and from what remained, he made toy trucks and trains to sell alongside the boats.

"The fen's earning its keep now, Dad," he said one chilly fall afternoon.

His father smiled and tossed scraps of wood into the stove. "I guess you would be right, boy."

Joe nurtured the orchids through spring floods and summer droughts, through fall storms and winter's arctic blasts, and against generations of industrious beavers. As he worked, he grew into a man with a family of his own. He inherited the farm and the land he cherished, even though he would never be a good farmer. He preferred woodworking, maple syrup production, and helping the orchids thrive.

Gradually, his efforts brought rewards.

The Showy Lady's Slippers multiplied, their rhizomes spreading like veins through the peaty earth. Not all at once, but in clusters that became colonies, they spread with the doggedness of time ticking through the decades.

His sixtieth summer came around, and early one morning, Joe called upstairs to his last and only child living at home. "There's dawn in the Lady's Slippers, Rhodena."

Rhodena stirred out of bed, and soon she and her father were standing ankle-deep in the fen. Water snakes slithered about their legs, and a bald eagle soared high above their heads. Like her father, Rhodena didn't mind the snakes. She understood they were just part of nature's grand scheme.

They stood in silence enjoying the carpet of wild orchids spreading around them.

Then suddenly, Rhodena called out, "Jump, Dad!" and they leapt into the air, quick as dragonflies. When they hit the ground again, the earth and every living thing around them jumped up. Rhodena squealed with delight.

The earth settled down and the fen grew still once more.

"How many slippers do you think there are today?" Rhodena asked.

A sly smile sneaked across her father's lined face. "More than there are bugs in the bush."

Rhodena squealed with delight and leapt into the air again. Joe leapt, too, whistling through his teeth. And they kept on jumping, squealing and whistling, even when their legs slipped out from under them and they plunked down in the murky earth, thrashing about like two creatures from an ancient bog.

EPILOGUE

Over the next seven years, Joe and Rhodena continued to nurture the Showy Lady's Slippers and several thousand more plants grew in the fen.

Word spread of the rare wild orchids on Purdon's farm, and every year more and more people came to see them in bloom. Joe and Rhodena welcomed anyone who knocked on the farmhouse door.

One winter's day, when snow lay several feet deep, Joe quietly passed away.

A short time later, his family honored his wish, entrusting the sixteen thousand Showy Lady's Slippers to the county's conservation authority, to ensure that the colony would prosper forever. Walkways were built to protect the orchids and to keep visitors from sinking into the spongy earth.

Today, if you visit, you might encounter Rhodena.

Say, "Hey," and ask her, "How many slippers are in bloom now?"

She might reply, "It's the largest colony in Canada and possibly North America."

And she would be right.

Born in 1914, Joe Purdon was a self-taught naturalist. He became one of Canada's earliest and mostly unheralded conservationists at a time when taking care of the land wasn't a part of the average citizen's awareness, nor had it become part of the Canadian consciousness. From that fateful day when he stumbled upon a cluster of Showy Lady's Slippers in bloom, Joe was the steward of a fragile piece of family land deep in the Lanark Highlands of Eastern Ontario. A national treasure emerged due to his passion and vigilance over more than five decades.

Purdon Conservation Area, now the Mississippi Valley Conservation Authority, was established in 1982 to protect the rare wild orchids because of the generosity and vision of one man.